MW00699321

THIS PLANNER BELONGS TO:

_____

BOOK LOVERS!

Here you will find the reading planner you've always dreamed of. This twelve-month reading journey invites you to explore some must-read titles selected by the American Library Association and keep track of your personal reading list. Set reading goals, track your progress, and proudly check off the books you read. Fun extras throughout, including inspiring quotes, a place for reflection and notes, and plenty of space to update your likely never-ending to-be-read list make this planner a reading adventure you'll cherish, week after week.

Are you ready to read?

MY READING CHALLENGE FAVORITES

NOTE YOUR FAVORITES ON THE SPINES

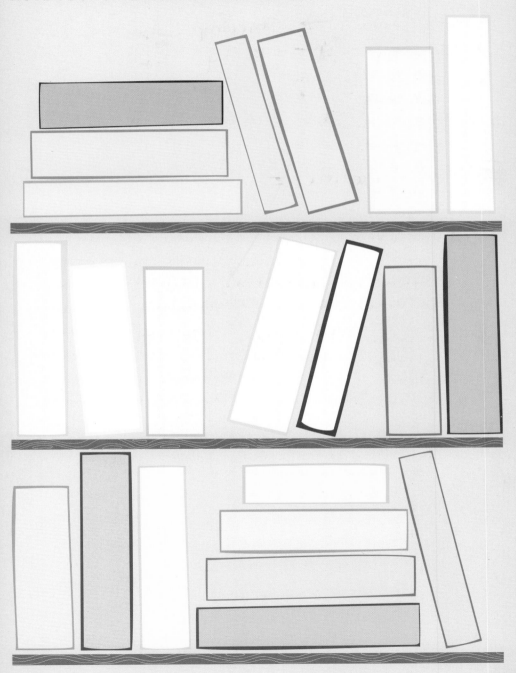

MONTH & YEAR: January 2025

SUNDAY	MONDAY	TUESDAY	WEDNESDAY
• Maria Ines → Shipping → ○ Receiving ← Karly → • Xesenia → Shipphg → Receiving • ~~Xime~~ ← Ximena			
☰ Mas practica ☰ ☰ Tarea ☰			
1. Revisar al personal respecto politicas de vestimenta 2. Revisar la parte de cajas y los libros de			

THURSDAY	FRIDAY	SATURDAY

MONTHLY GOALS

GOALS FOR THE MONTH AHEAD

WHAT WORKED LAST MONTH

FAVORITE BOOKS AND MOMENTS FROM LAST MONTH

READING IS HABIT

TRACK NEW HABITS & READING GOALS AND WATCH YOUR PROGRESS EVERY MONTH!

HABIT	1	2	3	4	5	6	7	8	9	10	11	12	13	14	15	16	17	18	19	20	21	22	23	24	25	26	27	28	29	30	31

AMERICANAH

CHIMAMANDA NGOZI ADICHIE

ANDREW CARNEGIE MEDAL FOR EXCELLENCE IN FICTION, 2014 FINALIST

DATE STARTED	DATE FINISHED	MY RATING
		☆☆☆☆☆

To the women in the hair-braiding salon, Ifemelu seems to have everything a Nigerian immigrant in America could desire, but the culture shock, hardships, and racism she's endured have left her feeling like she has "cement in her soul." Smart, irreverent, and outspoken, she reluctantly left Nigeria on a college scholarship. Her aunty Uju, the pampered mistress of a general in Lagos, is now struggling on her own in the United States, trying to secure her medical license. Ifemelu's discouraging job search brings on desperation and depression until a babysitting gig leads to a cashmere-and-champagne romance with a wealthy white man. Astonished at the labyrinthine racial strictures she's confronted with, Ifemelu, defining herself as a "Non-American Black," launches an audacious, provocative, and instantly popular blog in which she explores what she calls Racial Disorder Syndrome. Meanwhile, her abandoned true love, Obinze, is suffering his own cold miseries as an unwanted African in London.

Describe the communities that you are a part of and why they are important to you.

THE WEEK OF _____ – _____

MON

TUE

WED

THU

FRI

SAT

SUN

"There are many different ways to be poor
in the world but increasingly there seems
to be one single way to be rich."

CHIMAMANDA NGOZI ADICHIE, *AMERICANAH*

HOMELAND ELEGIES

AYAD AKHTAR

ANDREW CARNEGIE MEDAL FOR EXCELLENCE IN FICTION, 2021 FINALIST

DATE STARTED	DATE FINISHED	MY RATING
		☆☆☆☆☆

This memoiristic tale about a young Pakistani American before and after 9/11 is not truly a novel in the usual sense, but rather a series of linked short stories reflecting on author Ayad Akhtar's experiences as the child of Muslim immigrants and his place in American society. A common thread is his relationship with his father, Sikander, initially a superfan of Donald Trump and all things American, and his growing disillusionment with his adopted country. Akhtar's mother, homesick for Pakistan and critical of American materialism, presents a quiet rebuke to his father's hyper patriotism, as do various Pakistani relatives and family friends. As Akhtar comes of age, he interacts with an array of fascinating characters with different insights into the American character: an anti-capitalist literature professor, a Pakistani hedge-fund billionaire determined to become the Muslim Sheldon Adelson, and an African American Republican who wants to defund the racist government.

In your own coming-of-age story, who are the family and friends that influenced you the most?

THE WEEK OF _____ – _____

MON

TUE

WED

THU

FRI

SAT

SUN

"A day spent reading is not a great day.
But a life spent reading is a wonderful life."

AYAD AKHTAR, *HOMELAND ELEGIES*

THE HOUSE OF THE SPIRITS

ISABEL ALLENDE

3

DATE STARTED	DATE FINISHED	MY RATING
		☆☆☆☆☆

In this debut novel, author Isabel Allende, niece of Chilean president Salvador Allende, who was slain in the military coup of 1973, has written a compelling family chronicle. Patriarch Esteban dreams of politics and his clairvoyant wife, Clara. Their daughter, Blanca, infuriates her father by falling deeply in love with the peasant Pedro. Alba, beloved granddaughter of Esteban and daughter of Blanca and Pedro, is a revolutionary who leads the family into a hopeful future. Allende's portrait of the Trueba clan and her picture of an unnamed country's political history create a splendid and fantastic meditation on a people and a nation victimized and brutalized by their past.

Who are the key characters in your family chronicle?
How would you describe each of them?

THE WEEK OF ______ – ______

MON

TUE

WED

THU

FRI

SAT

SUN

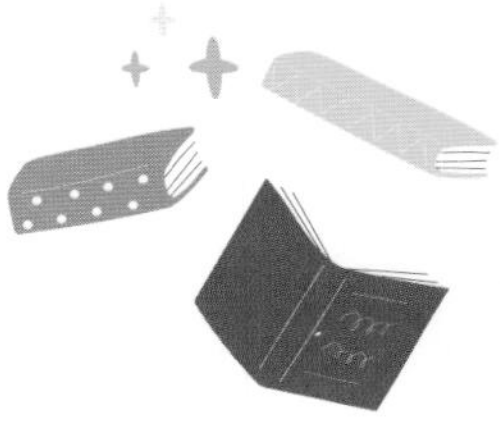

"You can't find someone who doesn't want to be found."

ISABEL ALLENDE, *THE HOUSE OF THE SPIRITS*

FUN HOME:
A FAMILY TRAGICOMIC
ALISON BECHDEL

4

DATE STARTED	DATE FINISHED	MY RATING
		☆☆☆☆☆

This autobiographical coming out story is largely about father and daughter. Author Alison Bechdel's mother and two brothers are in it, of course, but her father, Bruce Bechdel, had the biggest impact on his eldest child and so is naturally the other main character in her graphic novel. After Alison disclosed her lesbianism in a letter home from college, her mother replied that her father was homosexual too. Alison suddenly understood his legal trouble over buying a beer for a teenage boy, all the teen male "helpers" he had around the house, and his solo outings during family vacations to New York. This memoir, which uses her childhood journals as a source, speaks eloquently to the psychological and social battles fought and left unfought in this fraught family dynamic.

Describe a memory centered on your father.

THE WEEK OF _____ — _____

MON

TUE

WED

THU

FRI

SAT　　　　　　　　　　　　　　　　　　　　　　　　　　　　　　**SUN**

"It was not a triumphal return.
Home, as I had known it, was gone."

ALISON BECHDEL, *FUN HOME*

5

THE FIREBRAND AND THE FIRST LADY: PORTRAIT OF A FRIENDSHIP: PAULI MURRAY, ELEANOR ROOSEVELT, AND THE STRUGGLE FOR SOCIAL JUSTICE

PATRICIA BELL-SCOTT

ANDREW CARNEGIE MEDAL FOR EXCELLENCE IN NONFICTION, 2017 FINALIST

DATE STARTED	DATE FINISHED	MY RATING
		☆☆☆☆☆

Eleanor Roosevelt, born to privilege, prosperity, and power, first crossed paths with Pauli Murray, the granddaughter of an enslaved woman struggling against racism and poverty, in 1934 when the First Lady visited an upstate New York facility for unemployed women. Murray was in residence after fleeing the Jim Crow South to put herself through college in Manhattan. Four years later, Murray sent the opening salvo in what became a fervent correspondence that lasted until Roosevelt's death, as these two brilliant, courageous, committed trailblazers—both orphaned young, taunted for their appearance, devoted to reading and writing, boundlessly energetic, and fiercely independent—joined forces to fight for justice and equality.

Write about a friendship that has altered the course of your life.

THE WEEK OF _____ – _____

MON

TUE

WED

THU

FRI

SAT

SUN

"She hammered the keys with
the focus of a prizefighter."

PATRICIA BELL-SCOTT,
THE FIREBRAND AND THE FIRST LADY

MONTH & YEAR: _____

SUNDAY	MONDAY	TUESDAY	WEDNESDAY

THURSDAY	FRIDAY	SATURDAY

MONTHLY GOALS

GOALS FOR THE MONTH AHEAD

WHAT WORKED LAST MONTH

FAVORITE BOOKS AND MOMENTS FROM LAST MONTH

READING IS HABIT

TRACK NEW HABITS & READING GOALS AND WATCH YOUR PROGRESS EVERY MONTH!

HABIT	1	2	3	4	5	6	7	8	9	10	11	12	13	14	15	16	17	18	19	20	21	22	23	24	25	26	27	28	29	30	31

6

FIREKEEPER'S DAUGHTER
ANGELINE BOULLEY

DATE STARTED	DATE FINISHED	MY RATING
		☆☆☆☆☆

Reeling after the death of her uncle, Daunis is trying to adjust to her new normal, a challenge at the best of times in her gossip-prone town, especially when her scandalous origins leave her caught between two worlds—Ojibwe on her father's side but not officially enrolled as a member of the tribe, and French, dating back to fur traders, on the side of her mother, who considers the other half of Daunis's heritage a defect. When she witnesses a murder at the hands of someone who is addicted to meth and from a prominent family of her tribe, she has a choice: let the cycle of pain continue or protect her community.

Describe a difficult choice you had to make.

THE WEEK OF _____ — _____

MON

TUE

WED

THU

FRI

SAT

SUN

"Kindness is something that seems small, Daunis,
but it's like tossing a pebble into a pond and
the ripples reach further than you thought."

ANGELINE BOULLEY, *FIREKEEPER'S DAUGHTER*

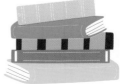

THE WATER DANCER

TA-NEHISI COATES

ANDREW CARNEGIE MEDAL FOR EXCELLENCE IN FICTION, 2020 FINALIST

DATE STARTED	DATE FINISHED	MY RATING
		☆☆☆☆☆

Hiram Walker is the son of an enslaved woman and her slave master, owner of a prominent Virginia estate. When Hiram is nearly killed in a drowning accident, he detects an amazing gift he cannot understand or harness. He travels between worlds, gone but not gone, and sees his mother, Rose, who was sold away when he was a child. Despite this astonishing vision, he cannot remember much about Rose. His power and his memory are major forces that propel Hiram into an adulthood filled with the hypocrisy of slavery, including the requisite playacting that flavors a stew of complex relationships. Struggling with his own longing for freedom, Hiram finds his affiliations tested with Thena, the taciturn old woman who took him in as a child; Sophia, a young woman fighting against her fate on the plantation; and Hiram's father, who obliquely acknowledges him as a son. Throughout his courageous journey north and participation in the underground battle for liberation, Hiram struggles to match his gift with his mission.

How do you match your gifts with your mission?

THE WEEK OF _____ — _____

MON

TUE

WED

THU

FRI

SAT

SUN

"What you must now accept is that all of
us are bound to something... All must name
a master to serve. All must choose."

TA-NEHISI COATES, *THE WATER DANCER*

8

RAZORBLADE TEARS
S. A. COSBY

DATE STARTED	DATE FINISHED	MY RATING
		☆☆☆☆☆

Ike Randolph and Buddy Lee Jenkins, both ex-cons, have little else in common. Ike is a Black man who has built his own landscaping business since leaving jail; Buddy Lee is an alcoholic redneck and casual racist who lives in a ramshackle trailer. What brings them together is the brutal murder of their sons, who were married to one another. Neither Ike nor Buddy Lee could overcome their ingrained homophobia while their sons were alive, but now they want revenge and come together to find the killers. As these two self-acknowledged "bad men" reacquaint themselves with their instincts for perpetrating extreme violence, they also begin to learn about their own prejudices. "Being who you are shouldn't be a goddamn death sentence," Ike says, even as he hopes to carry out that very sentence against the men who killed his son.

**Write about an unexpected event that compelled you
to join forces with someone unlike yourself.**

THE WEEK OF _____ – _____

MON

TUE

WED

THU

FRI

SAT

SUN

"When the people you love are gone,
it's the things they've touched that
keep them alive in your mind."

S. A. COSBY, *RAZORBLADE TEARS*

9

EVICTED: POVERTY AND PROFIT IN THE AMERICAN CITY

MATTHEW DESMOND

ANDREW CARNEGIE MEDAL FOR EXCELLENCE IN NONFICTION, 2017 WINNER

DATE STARTED	DATE FINISHED	MY RATING
		☆☆☆☆☆

It is difficult to paint a slumlord as an even remotely sympathetic character, but Harvard professor Matthew Desmond manages to do so in this compelling look at home evictions in Milwaukee, Wisconsin, one of America's most segregated cities. Two landlords are profiled here: Sherrena, who owns dozens of dilapidated units on Milwaukee's infamous North Side, and Tobin, who runs a trailer park on the South Side. They are in it to make money, to be sure, but they also have a tendency to rent to those in need and to look the other way. More often than not, however, they find themselves hauling tenants to eviction court, and here we meet eight families. Among them are Arleen, a single mother dragging her two youngest sons across town in urgent search of a warm, safe place; Scott, a drug addict desperate to crawl up from rock bottom; and Larraine, who loses all of her belongings when she's evicted.

How does your home reflect your personality, values, and aspirations?

THE WEEK OF _____ — _____

MON

TUE

WED

THU

FRI

SAT

SUN

"The home remains the primary basis of life.
It is where meals are shared, quiet habits
formed, dreams confessed, traditions created."

MATTHEW DESMOND, *EVICTED*

MONTH & YEAR: _____

SUNDAY	MONDAY	TUESDAY	WEDNESDAY

THURSDAY	FRIDAY	SATURDAY

MONTHLY GOALS

GOALS FOR THE MONTH AHEAD

WHAT WORKED LAST MONTH

FAVORITE BOOKS AND MOMENTS FROM LAST MONTH

READING IS HABIT

TRACK NEW HABITS & READING GOALS AND WATCH YOUR PROGRESS EVERY MONTH!

HABIT	1	2	3	4	5	6	7	8	9	10	11	12	13	14	15	16	17	18	19	20	21	22	23	24	25	26	27	28	29	30	31

ALL THE LIGHT WE CANNOT SEE

ANTHONY DOERR

ANDREW CARNEGIE MEDAL FOR EXCELLENCE IN FICTION, 2015 WINNER

DATE STARTED	DATE FINISHED	MY RATING
		☆☆☆☆☆

Marie-Louise is a sightless girl who lived with her father in Paris before the occupation of France during WWII; her father was a master locksmith for the Museum of Natural History. When German forces necessitate abandonment of the city, Marie-Louise's father, taking with him the museum's greatest treasure, removes himself and his daughter and eventually arrives at his uncle's house in the coastal city of Saint-Malo. Young German soldier Werner, on the opposite side of the conflagration that is destroying Europe, is sent to Saint-Malo to track Resistance activity there, and eventually—and inevitably—Marie-Louise's and Werner's paths cross.

If you had to abandon your city, what would you take with you?

THE WEEK OF _____ – _____

MON

TUE

WED

THU

FRI

SAT

SUN

"Time is a slippery thing: lose hold
of it once, and its string might
sail out of your hands forever."

ANTHONY DOERR, *ALL THE LIGHT WE CANNOT SEE*

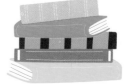

WASHINGTON BLACK

ESI EDUGYAN

ANDREW CARNEGIE MEDAL FOR EXCELLENCE IN FICTION, 2019 FINALIST

11

DATE STARTED	DATE FINISHED	MY RATING
		☆☆☆☆☆

The year 1830 finds eleven-year-old George Washington ("Wash") Black enslaved on a sugar plantation in Barbados. His life changes dramatically when his master's younger brother, Titch, chooses Wash to assist with his scientific experiments. When an innocent Wash is in danger of being charged with a death, he and Titch flee in a hot-air balloon of Titch's design. The balloon comes to ruin, but the two survive to journey to the Arctic, where they hope to determine if Titch's renowned scientist father is still alive. It is there that Titch abandons Wash. The boy, by now thirteen and a gifted artist, makes his way to Nova Scotia where he meets the daughter of an eminent zoologist. The three journey to London, where Wash begins to make it his business to find Titch, if he is still alive.

What opportunities have you been given that changed your life for the better?

THE WEEK OF _____ – _____

MON

TUE

WED

THU

FRI

SAT

SUN

"Be faithful to what you see, Washington,
and not to what you are supposed to see."

ESI EDUGYAN, *WASHINGTON BLACK*

MANHATTAN BEACH

JENNIFER EGAN

ANDREW CARNEGIE MEDAL FOR EXCELLENCE IN FICTION, 2018 WINNER

DATE STARTED	DATE FINISHED	MY RATING
		☆☆☆☆☆

In 1934, eleven-year-old Anna Kerrigan accompanies her father, Eddie, a union bagman, on a trip to the seaside home of mobster Dexter Styles. Dexter, a dashing and ruthless nightclub impresario, is impressed with Anna's urge to walk barefoot in the frigid sand and sea. "Well, what's it feel like?" he asks. "It only hurts at first," she says. "After a while you can't feel anything." Her father is not pleased, but Dexter grins and says, "Words to live by." Ten years later, her father is gone, and Anna joins the war effort, securing a job at the Brooklyn Naval Yard inspecting parts for battleships. She has an epiphany while watching a man don a massive diving suit: she is destined to be a diver. Her wildly unconventional conviction carries her over every obstacle placed in her way. She also reconnects with Dexter Styles and attempts to discover the fate of her father. Anna does what she believes she must in her search for answers, hope, and ascension.

What did you dream of doing as a child?

THE WEEK OF _____ — _____

MON

TUE

WED

THU

FRI

SAT

SUN

"It brought a sense of returning to an earlier time when she was questioned more often and had fewer evasions at her disposal."

JENNIFER EGAN, *MANHATTAN BEACH*

THE FORGOTTEN WALTZ

ANNE ENRIGHT

ANDREW CARNEGIE MEDAL FOR EXCELLENCE IN FICTION, 2012 WINNER

DATE STARTED	DATE FINISHED	MY RATING
		☆☆☆☆☆

Gina Moynihan is married, holds a professional business position, and is now recalling an obsessive, selfish, and problem-riddled affair with the equally married Sean Vallely. Gina remembers that affair not in chronological order but in fits and starts only, eventually concluding at the end. Here is a story of the vicissitudes, obstructions, and collateral damage of an adulterous affair in a milieu rife with mixed feelings and muddled dreams.

Describe your most intense emotional experience.

THE WEEK OF _____ – _____

MON

TUE

WED

THU

FRI

SAT

SUN

"Who would have thought love
could be so expensive?"

ANNE ENRIGHT, *THE FORGOTTEN WALTZ*

14

THE SENTENCE
LOUISE ERDRICH

DATE STARTED	DATE FINISHED	MY RATING
		☆☆☆☆☆

Birchbark Books, a Minneapolis-based bookstore, is haunted. The unhappy spirit is that of a former customer, Flora, who irritated the Native staff members, especially Tookie, with her dubious claims of an Indigenous heritage. Tookie is supremely dedicated to her work, forever amazed, given her prison record, to have been hired by store owner Louise. While she seems tough and ornery, Tookie is actually quite "porous" emotionally and suffused with love for her tribal leader husband, Pollux, in spite of their complicated past. As Tookie tries to appease Flora, she and her bookstore colleagues—a teacher, a historian, and an artist—confront historic ghosts from the violent seizing of the land by white settlers as the fear and sorrow of the COVID-19 pandemic takes hold and the city ignites in the wake of George Floyd's murder by a Minneapolis police officer.

**Write about something that haunts you—
a ghost, an object, or an idea.**

THE WEEK OF _____ — _____

MON

TUE

WED

THU

FRI

SAT

SUN

"The world was filling with ghosts.
We were a haunted country in a haunted world."

LOUISE ERDRICH, *THE SENTENCE*

MONTH & YEAR: _____

SUNDAY	MONDAY	TUESDAY	WEDNESDAY

THURSDAY	FRIDAY	SATURDAY

MONTHLY GOALS

GOALS FOR THE MONTH AHEAD

WHAT WORKED LAST MONTH

FAVORITE BOOKS AND MOMENTS FROM LAST MONTH

READING IS HABIT

TRACK NEW HABITS & READING GOALS AND WATCH YOUR PROGRESS EVERY MONTH!

HABIT	1	2	3	4	5	6	7	8	9	10	11	12	13	14	15	16	17	18	19	20	21	22	23	24	25	26	27	28	29	30	31

15

CANADA

RICHARD FORD

ANDREW CARNEGIE MEDAL FOR EXCELLENCE IN FICTION, 2013 WINNER

DATE STARTED	DATE FINISHED	MY RATING
		☆☆☆☆☆

After fifteen-year-old Dell Parsons's parents rob a bank and are arrested, the trajectory of his life is forever altered. He and his twin sister, Berner, are left to forge their own futures while still reeling from the shock of their parents' desperate act. Berner, burning with resentment, takes off for the West Coast, while a family friend makes arrangements for Dell to hide in Canada. But what Dell discovers in Canada while in the employ of a mysterious Harvard-educated American with a violent streak is to take nothing for granted, for "every pillar of the belief the world rests on may or may not be about to explode." Dell not only survives his traumatic adolescence but manages to thrive, while Berner, seemingly more worldly, succumbs to drink and a fractured existence.

What family decision has shifted the trajectory of your life?

THE WEEK OF _____ — _____

MON

TUE

WED

THU

FRI

SAT

SUN

"Every pillar of the belief the world rests on
may or may not be about to explode."

RICHARD FORD, CANADA

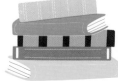

16

FATHOMS: THE WORLD IN THE WHALE

REBECCA GIGGS

ANDREW CARNEGIE MEDAL FOR EXCELLENCE IN NONFICTION, 2021 FINALIST

DATE STARTED	DATE FINISHED	MY RATING
		☆☆☆☆☆

Fathoms evokes depth both as a unit of measurement for bodies of water and as "an attempt to understand," writes author Rebecca Giggs. She then takes sea soundings by focusing on the history and current plight of whales, beginning with a beached humpback whale on her home ground in Perth, Australia. Giggs punctuates this encompassing cetacean chronicle with lists of human-generated objects found in dead whales' digestive systems. Even more alarming is how saturated whales are with toxic chemicals: "Inside the whale, the world." With fresh perceptions and cascades of facts, Giggs considers our ancient and persistent whale wonderment, high-tech whale hunting, the 1970s Save the Whales movement, global warming, mass extinction, and pollution, including the oceanic plastic plague. She offers a startling assessment of how smartphones pose new perils for the wild and ponders the loss to our inner lives if we destroy the mystery of the sea. Giggs urges us to save the whales once again, and the oceans, and ourselves.

What do wild places and wild creatures mean to you?

THE WEEK OF _____ – _____

MON

TUE

WED

THU

FRI

SAT

SUN

"We are all tumbled together, human and nonhuman, the far and the nearby, deeply in torsion, inhabiting this change of state."

REBECCA GIGGS, *FATHOMS: THE WORLD IN THE WHALE*

17

KILLERS OF THE FLOWER MOON: THE OSAGE MURDERS AND THE BIRTH OF THE FBI

DAVID GRANN

ANDREW CARNEGIE MEDAL FOR EXCELLENCE IN NONFICTION, 2018 FINALIST

DATE STARTED	DATE FINISHED	MY RATING
		☆☆☆☆☆

During the early 1920s, many members of the Osage Indian Nation were murdered, one by one. After being forced from several homelands, the Osage had settled in the late nineteenth century in an unoccupied area of Oklahoma, chosen precisely because it was "rocky, sterile, and utterly unfit for cultivation." No white man would covet this land; Osage people would be happy. Then oil was discovered below the Osage territory, speedily attracting prospectors wielding staggering sums and turning many Osage into some of the richest people in the world. This true-crime mystery centers on Mollie Burkhart, an Osage woman who lost several family members as the death tally grew, and Tom White, the former Texas Ranger whom J. Edgar Hoover sent to solve the slippery, attention-grabbing case once and for all.

What mystery in your life (or in your family history) would you like to resolve?

THE WEEK OF _____ – _____

MON

TUE

WED

THU

FRI

SAT

SUN

"We gather the past and present into the depths of our being and face tomorrow."

DAVID GRANN, *KILLERS OF THE FLOWER MOON*

THE AUTOBIOGRAPHY OF MALCOLM X AS TOLD TO ALEX HALEY

MALCOLM X AND ALEX HALEY

DATE STARTED	DATE FINISHED	MY RATING
		☆☆☆☆☆

Malcolm X, an influential and controversial Black Muslim figure, relates his transformation from street hustler to religious and national leader in this first-person account. Born Malcolm Little, he moved to Michigan at age six after his father was killed by white supremacists. He spent years in foster homes, then as a drug dealer and pimp in New York and Boston. While in prison, he converted and joined the Nation of Islam, changed his name, and quickly became a leader in the organization. He later left the Nation of Islam but continued as an activist. Malcolm X was assassinated in February 1965, and this book—a collaboration between Malcolm and journalist Alex Haley—was published later that year.

Describe a cause you believe in.

MON

TUE

WED

THU

FRI

SAT

SUN

"Hence I have no mercy or compassion in me for a society that will crush people, and then penalize them for not being able to stand up under the weight."

MALCOLM X, *THE AUTOBIOGRAPHY OF MALCOLM X*

MONTH & YEAR: _____

SUNDAY	MONDAY	TUESDAY	WEDNESDAY

THURSDAY	FRIDAY	SATURDAY

MONTHLY GOALS

GOALS FOR THE MONTH AHEAD

WHAT WORKED LAST MONTH

FAVORITE BOOKS AND MOMENTS FROM LAST MONTH

READING IS HABIT

TRACK NEW HABITS & READING GOALS AND WATCH YOUR PROGRESS EVERY MONTH!

HABIT	1	2	3	4	5	6	7	8	9	10	11	12	13	14	15	16	17	18	19	20	21	22	23	24	25	26	27	28	29	30	31

19

MIDNIGHT IN CHERNOBYL: THE UNTOLD STORY OF THE WORLD'S GREATEST NUCLEAR DISASTER

ADAM HIGGINBOTHAM

ANDREW CARNEGIE MEDAL FOR EXCELLENCE IN NONFICTION, 2020 WINNER

DATE STARTED	DATE FINISHED	MY RATING
		☆☆☆☆☆

Midnight in Chernobyl is a top-notch historical narrative: a tense, fast-paced, engrossing, and revelatory product of more than a decade of research. Author Adam Higginbotham interviewed most of the surviving central participants in the disaster, examined volumes of newly declassified Soviet documents, and surveyed previous research and reportage. The result is a stunningly detailed account of the explosion of Reactor Four at the Chernobyl nuclear power plant on April 26, 1986. It offers a brief history of the development of the Soviet nuclear power program leading up to the construction of the plant at Chernobyl, a second-by-second account of the night of the accident, the confluence of causes, the evacuation of the surrounding countryside, the containment and cleanup efforts, and a deep dive into the aftermath: the medical and environmental consequences, the political machinations and missteps, the role Chernobyl played in the downfall of the USSR, and the effect it had on the pursuit of nuclear power worldwide. Higginbotham humanizes the tale, maintaining a focus on the people involved and the choices they made, both heroic and not, in unimaginable circumstances.

Describe a heroic action you took to help others.

THE WEEK OF _____ — _____

MON

TUE

WED

THU

FRI

SAT

SUN

"People won't understand if we do nothing...
We have to be seen to be doing something."

LEGASOV AS QUOTED BY ADAM HIGGINBOTHAM,
MIDNIGHT IN CHERNOBYL

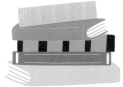

THE KITE RUNNER

KHALED HOSSEINI

DATE STARTED	DATE FINISHED	MY RATING
		☆☆☆☆☆

This story opens in Kabul in the mid-1970s. Amir is the son of a wealthy man, but his best friend is Hassan, the son of one of his father's servants. His father encourages the friendship and dotes on Hassan, who worships the ground Amir walks on. But Amir is envious of Hassan and his own father's apparent affection for the boy. One day, when Amir comes across a group of local bullies sexually assaulting Hassan, he does nothing. Shamed by his own inaction, Amir pushes Hassan away, even going so far as to accuse him of stealing. Eventually, Hassan and his father are forced to leave the country. Years later, Amir, now living in America, receives a visit from an old family friend who gives him an opportunity to make amends for his treatment of Hassan.

Write about a time you made amends.

THE WEEK OF _____ — _____

MON

TUE

WED

THU

FRI

SAT

SUN

"For you, a thousand times over."
KHALED HOSSEINI, *THE KITE RUNNER*

21

DEMON COPPERHEAD

BARBARA KINGSOLVER

DATE STARTED	DATE FINISHED	MY RATING
		☆☆☆☆☆

"A kid is a terrible thing to be, in charge of nothing." So says young Damon Fields, who's destined to be known as Demon Copperhead, a hungry orphan in a snake-harboring holler in Lee County, Virginia, where meth and opioids kill and nearly everyone is just scraping by. With his red hair and the "light-green eyes of a Melungeon," Damon's a dead ringer for his dead father, whom he never met. More parent to his mother than she was to him, he's subjected to hellish foster situations after her death, forced into hard labor, including a stint in a tobacco field, which ignites one of many righteous indictments of greed and exploitation. Damon funnels his dreams into drawings of superheroes, art being one of his secret powers. After risking his life to find his irascible grandmother, he ends up living in unnerving luxury with Coach Winfield and his smart, caustic, motherless daughter.

Describe a trial by fire you experienced.
What made it worthwhile?

THE WEEK OF ______________ – ______________

MON

TUE

WED

THU

FRI

SAT

SUN

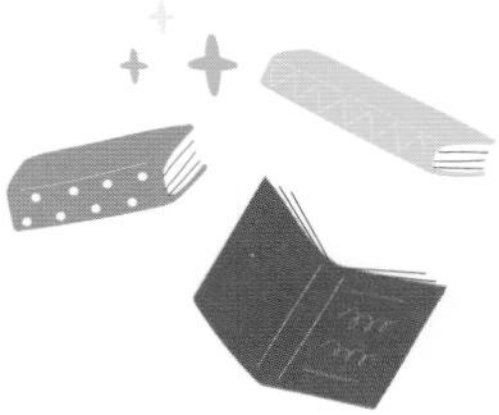

"The wonder is that you could start life with nothing, end with nothing, and lose so much in between."

BARBARA KINGSOLVER, *DEMON COPPERHEAD*

22

HEAVY: AN AMERICAN MEMOIR

KIESE LAYMON

ANDREW CARNEGIE MEDAL FOR EXCELLENCE IN NONFICTION, 2019 WINNER

DATE STARTED	DATE FINISHED	MY RATING
		☆☆☆☆☆

In his spectacular memoir, author Kiese Laymon recalls the traumas of his Mississippi youth. He captures his confusion at being molested by his babysitter and at witnessing older boys abuse a girl he liked; at having no food in the house despite his mother's brilliance; at being beaten and loved ferociously, often at the same time. His hungry mind and body grow until, like a flipping switch, at college he is compelled to shrink himself with a punishing combination of diet and exercise. Laymon applies his book's title to his body and his memories, to his inheritance as a student, a teacher, a writer, an activist, a Black man, and his mother's son—but also to the weight of truth and writing it.

What feels heavy in your life right now?
How does writing uplift you?

THE WEEK OF ____________________ – ____________________

MON

TUE

WED

THU

FRI

SAT

SUN

"I learned you haven't read anything if you've only read something once or twice. Reading things more than twice was the reader version of revision."

KIESE LAYMON, *HEAVY*

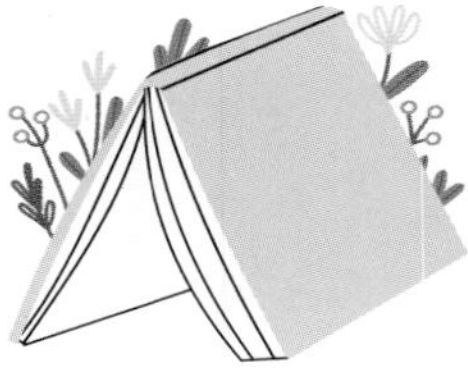

LOST CHILDREN ARCHIVE

VALERIA LUISELLI

ANDREW CARNEGIE MEDAL FOR EXCELLENCE IN FICTION, 2020 WINNER

DATE STARTED	DATE FINISHED	MY RATING
		☆☆☆☆☆

An unnamed couple and their children embark on a cross-country road trip from New York City to Arizona. Husband and wife both work as audio recording artists, dedicated to capturing the soundscapes of everyday life. Upon their arrival, he plans to investigate the native Apache people who used to populate the Southwest, and she has promised to find a friend's daughters who have been arrested at the border. When the family arrives at their destination, however, the overwhelming scale of the migrant crisis redirects their efforts, and the children eventually lose themselves in the strange, uncertain terrain. Husband and wife rush to recover their own offspring in this unsettling situation.

Describe a time in your life when you felt lost.

THE WEEK OF _____ – _____

MON

TUE

WED

THU

FRI

SAT

SUN

"Stories are a way of subtracting the
future from the past, the only way of
finding clarity in hindsight."

VALERIA LUISELLI, *LOST CHILDREN ARCHIVE*

MONTH & YEAR: _____

SUNDAY	MONDAY	TUESDAY	WEDNESDAY

THURSDAY	FRIDAY	SATURDAY

MONTHLY GOALS

GOALS FOR THE MONTH AHEAD

WHAT WORKED LAST MONTH

FAVORITE BOOKS AND MOMENTS FROM LAST MONTH

READING IS HABIT

TRACK NEW HABITS & READING GOALS AND WATCH YOUR PROGRESS EVERY MONTH!

HABIT	1	2	3	4	5	6	7	8	9	10	11	12	13	14	15	16	17	18	19	20	21	22	23	24	25	26	27	28	29	30	31

IN THE DREAM HOUSE: A MEMOIR

CARMEN MARIA MACHADO

DATE STARTED	DATE FINISHED	MY RATING
		☆☆☆☆☆

24

In this memoir, author Carmen Maria Machado chronicles her abusive relationship with a former partner, a slim blond woman who is referred to throughout as "the woman from the Dream House." The Dream House in question is the Bloomington, Indiana, home that Machado periodically spent time in during their long-distance relationship. She presents the story in fragments: "Dream House as Noir," "Dream House as Choose Your Own Adventure," "Dream House as Stoner Comedy," "Dream House as Entomology." In this way, she draws the reader deep into the varied rooms of the haunted house of the past.

What would you name the chapters in your life?

THE WEEK OF _____ – _____

MON

TUE

WED

THU

FRI

SAT

SUN

"We can't stop living. Which means we have
to live, which means we are alive, which
means we are humans and we are human."

CARMEN MARIA MACHADO, *IN THE DREAM HOUSE*

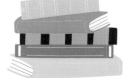

25

A BURNING

MEGHA MAJUMDAR

ANDREW CARNEGIE MEDAL FOR EXCELLENCE IN FICTION, 2021 FINALIST

DATE STARTED	DATE FINISHED	MY RATING
		☆☆☆☆☆

For the first time in her young life, Jivan has her own cell phone, which she bought with money earned by working as a shopgirl, having left high school after barely passing her tenth-form exams. After witnessing a gruesome train-station attack during her fifteen-minute walk home to the slums, she continues to follow events on Facebook. And then Jivan does "a foolish thing...a dangerous thing, immaturely hoping to multiply her 'likes' by responding to a post: if the police watched them die...doesn't that mean that the government is also a terrorist?" Days later, Jivan has been beaten and jailed, accused of terrorism, effectively condemned without a trial. The two people who could possibly save her—a trans woman to whom Jivan was attempting to teach English, and her former PE teacher, who recognized her athletic prowess—have other priorities: dreams of film stardom for Lovely, a political future for PT Sir. Still holding on to her innocence, Jivan entrusts her story to a hungry journalist. Salvation seems possible, even narrowly so, over and over again, until it's not.

What obstacles seem insurmountable in pursuit of your dreams?

MON

TUE

WED

THU

FRI

SAT

SUN

"But now I am knowing that there is no use asking these questions. In life, many things are happening for no reason at all."

MEGHA MAJUMDAR, *A BURNING*

I HAVE SOME QUESTIONS FOR YOU

REBECCA MAKKAI

DATE STARTED	DATE FINISHED	MY RATING
		☆☆☆☆☆

Bodie Kane, a successful podcaster and professor of film, goes back for a two-week stint to her old private high school in New Hampshire to teach classes on podcasting and film history. Her return awakens memories of friends—particularly her roommate, Thalia, who was murdered in her senior year. When one of her students decides to base her podcast on the crime, Bodie is forced to reexamine the facts.

Write about an unresolved issue from your past.

THE WEEK OF ______________ – ______________

MON

TUE

WED

THU

FRI

SAT

SUN

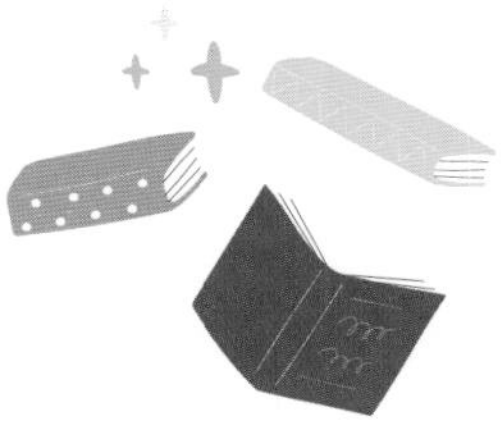

"Just because you can't picture someone doing something doesn't mean they aren't capable of it."

REBECCA MAKKAI, *I HAVE SOME QUESTIONS FOR YOU*

27

THE DAVENPORTS
KRYSTAL MARQUIS

DATE STARTED	DATE FINISHED	MY RATING
		☆☆☆☆☆

It's 1910, and in Chicago, the Davenports are one of the few Black families to achieve wealth and status. Formerly enslaved William Davenport runs a successful carriage company and searches futilely for the brother he was separated from when they escaped slavery. His three children are preoccupied with the present. Olivia, the perfect society girl, knows it's her responsibility to marry well, but as a handsome civil rights lawyer opens her eyes to the realities Black people face, she begins to wonder if there's more beyond her world. Her younger sister Helen's days spent fixing cars and dreaming of taking over their father's business are the worst-kept secret in town, until her sister's erstwhile suitor sweeps her off her feet. Their brother, John, is falling for Amy-Rose, the mixed-race maid saving up for her own shop and facing suspicion from the Black community for her lighter skin. And Ruby, Olivia's best friend, tries to win John's affections as her family's fortunes fail, but she may accidentally be falling for the man she's made her pawn.

**Write about the history of your neighborhood, town, or city.
Or make up a new historical narrative that takes place within it.**

MON

TUE

WED

THU

FRI

SAT

SUN

"Much of what affects our lives is out of our control.
We should always strive to make the choices we
can. Life is too short, too full of heartache."

KRYSTAL MARQUIS, *THE DAVENPORTS*

MONTH & YEAR: _____

SUNDAY	MONDAY	TUESDAY	WEDNESDAY

THURSDAY	FRIDAY	SATURDAY

MONTHLY GOALS

GOALS FOR THE MONTH AHEAD

WHAT WORKED LAST MONTH

FAVORITE BOOKS AND MOMENTS FROM LAST MONTH

READING IS HABIT

TRACK NEW HABITS & READING GOALS AND WATCH YOUR PROGRESS EVERY MONTH!

HABIT	1	2	3	4	5	6	7	8	9	10	11	12	13	14	15	16	17	18	19	20	21	22	23	24	25	26	27	28	29	30	31

CATHERINE THE GREAT: PORTRAIT OF A WOMAN

ROBERT K. MASSIE

ANDREW CARNEGIE MEDAL FOR EXCELLENCE IN NONFICTION, 2012 WINNER

28

DATE STARTED	DATE FINISHED	MY RATING
		☆☆☆☆☆

Sophie of Anhalt-Zerbst, as Catherine the Great was originally named, appeals to readers for several reasons. Those interested in the expansion and development of the Russian Empire under her reign (1762–96) can delve into her conduct of war and diplomacy, cultivation of Enlightenment notables, and attempted reforms of law and government, and those fascinated by the intimate intrigues of dynasties will find an extraordinary example in Catherine's ascent from minor German princess to absolute autocrat of Russia. Included is Catherine's own account of surviving palace politics as consort to the eccentric and disliked crown prince, Paul, and allusions to her liaisons with courtiers, most famously Grigory Potemkin. Massie humanizes the real woman behind the imperial persona.

Who are your favorite royals, and why?

THE WEEK OF _____ – _____

MON

TUE

WED

THU

FRI

SAT

SUN

"The love of power and the power to attract love were not easy to reconcile."

ROBERT K. MASSIE,
CATHERINE THE GREAT: PORTRAIT OF A WOMAN

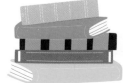

29

DEACON KING KONG

JAMES MCBRIDE

ANDREW CARNEGIE MEDAL FOR EXCELLENCE IN FICTION, 2021 WINNER

DATE STARTED	DATE FINISHED	MY RATING
		☆☆☆☆☆

On a cloudy September 1969 afternoon, septuagenarian widower Sportcoat—less respectfully dubbed Deacon King Kong for his addiction to the local moonshine—shot nineteen-year-old drug dealer Deems, then saved Deems's life with an unseemly version of the Heimlich maneuver when Deems nearly choked on his tuna sandwich. That shocking spectacle, which Sportcoat won't even remember, reverberates through South Brooklyn's Causeway Housing Projects and beyond...because everyone seems related by hook or by crook. While Sportcoat's dead wife continues to nag him regularly, his best friend tries to convince him to run for his life. Sportcoat claims innocence and refuses to flee, remembering Deems as the Projects' best pitcher on his way to a baseball scholarship just a year ago. Meanwhile, down on the piers, the Italian Elefante is trying to keep his shipments moving without taking on the expanding baggage of illegal drugs, but he's suddenly faced with fulfilling a promise his late father made to an aging Irish bagel maker.

**Describe one or more interesting characters
in your neighborhood and what motivates them.**

THE WEEK OF _____ – _____

MON

TUE

WED

THU

FRI

SAT

SUN

"Most times I don't know what I'm doing.
Sometimes I feel like I don't hardly
know enough to tie my own shoes."

JAMES MCBRIDE, *DEACON KING KONG*

30

RADIUM GIRLS: THE DARK STORY OF AMERICA'S SHINING WOMEN

KATE MOORE

DATE STARTED	DATE FINISHED	MY RATING
		☆☆☆☆☆

In 1917, the Radium Luminous Materials Corporation willingly employed young women, paid far better than most businesses, and had many enticing perks—including the glow. Radium girls, most in their teens and early twenties, painted watch dials with a luminescent paint mixed with radium dust, which clung to their hair and clothes and produced a telltale glow about them as they walked home each evening. At the time, radium was used in cancer treatments and touted in expensive tonics, so the girls didn't question smoothing the radium-laden paint-brushes in their mouths, as instructed, or even painting their nails with them. But the women would soon suffer horrific pain and grotesquely shattered bones and teeth, and the company, it would be discovered, had known better. In 1928, just eight years after women had earned the right to vote, a group of former radium girls sued the companies whose knowledge of radium's hazards and careless disregard for them had endangered and harmed them.

Describe an act of resistance that inspires you.

MON

TUE

WED

THU

FRI

SAT

SUN

"Radium, he determined, was dangerous.
It was just that nobody told the girls."

KATE MOORE, *THE RADIUM GIRLS*

31

MY YEAR OF REST AND RELAXATION

OTTESSA MOSHFEGH

DATE STARTED	DATE FINISHED	MY RATING
		☆☆☆☆☆

An unnamed twenty-four-year-old narrator decides to hibernate in 2000. For about a year, aided by a dizzying parade of pills, she'll treat the Manhattan apartment her inheritance bought her as her den. Her occasional boyfriend treats her horribly, her only friend, Reva, annoys her, and her job working in a Chelsea gallery is literally tiresome: she spends part of every workday napping in a supply closet. None of this is new though; she has just finally made up her mind to embrace the slumber she so craves. As her medications' effectiveness begins to wane, she invents symptoms and increasingly disturbing dreams to elicit ever-stronger medications from her dubiously qualified doctor, until she lands on Infermiterol. Just one pill took "days of my life away. It was the perfect drug in that sense." Amidst her haze, the narrator recalls her dead parents—her mother, especially, resembles a fairy-tale villain—and doesn't disguise her inability to empathize with Reva, whose own mother is dying.

Describe a strong emotion you've experienced using sensory details and specific imagery.

THE WEEK OF _____ – _____

MON

TUE

WED

THU

FRI

SAT

SUN

"The notion of my future suddenly
snapped into focus: it didn't exist yet."

OTTESSA MOSHFEGH, *MY YEAR OF REST AND RELAXATION*

32

HOW HIGH WE GO IN THE DARK

SEQUOIA NAGAMATSU

DATE STARTED	DATE FINISHED	MY RATING
		☆☆☆☆☆

Dr. Cliff Miyashiro journeys to Siberia to finish the work that claimed the life of his daughter, a passionate environmentalist. When Cliff and his colleagues accidentally release an ancient virus contained in the remains of a prehistoric girl frozen in ice, the world christens it the Arctic plague. As the pandemic spreads across the earth, society finds ways to grieve and honor the dying and dead, including erecting an amusement park specifically for terminally ill children, creating robotic dogs that capture the voices and personalities of lost loved ones, and establishing hotels where families can stay to celebrate the lives of those they've lost. The tragedy causes humanity to look to the stars for salvation, as Cliff's wife, Miki, sets off with their granddaughter and a contingent of pioneers hoping to establish a colony on a habitable planet.

**Write about connecting with the ones you love.
How do you show them you care from afar?**

THE WEEK OF _____ — _____

MON

TUE

WED

THU

FRI

SAT

SUN

"Hope, love, ingenuity. Possibility is more than
what runs through our veins, little one."

SEQUOIA NAGAMATSU, *HOW HIGH WE GO IN THE DARK*

MONTH & YEAR: _____

SUNDAY	MONDAY	TUESDAY	WEDNESDAY

THURSDAY	FRIDAY	SATURDAY

MONTHLY GOALS

GOALS FOR THE MONTH AHEAD

WHAT WORKED LAST MONTH

FAVORITE BOOKS AND MOMENTS FROM LAST MONTH

READING IS HABIT

TRACK NEW HABITS & READING GOALS AND WATCH YOUR PROGRESS EVERY MONTH!

HABIT	1	2	3	4	5	6	7	8	9	10	11	12	13	14	15	16	17	18	19	20	21	22	23	24	25	26	27	28	29	30	31

THE SYMPATHIZER

VIET THANH NGUYEN

ANDREW CARNEGIE MEDAL FOR EXCELLENCE IN FICTION, 2016 WINNER

33

DATE STARTED	DATE FINISHED	MY RATING
		☆☆☆☆☆

Adept in the merciless art of interrogation, the nameless spy who narrates this dark novel knows how to pry answers from the unwilling. Unexpectedly, however, this Vietnamese Communist sympathizer finds himself being tortured by the very revolutionary zealots he has helped make victorious in Saigon. He responds to this torture by extending an intense self-interrogation already underway before his incarceration. The narrator thus plumbs his singular double-mindedness by reliving his turbulent life as the bastard son of a French priest and a devout Asian mother. Haunted by a faith he no longer accepts, insecure in the Communist ideology he has embraced, the spy sweeps a vision sharpened by disillusion-ment across the tangled individual psyches of those close to him—a friend, a lover, a comrade—and into the warped motives of the imperialists and ideologues governing the world he must navigate.

How have your beliefs changed over time?

THE WEEK OF _____ – _____

MON

TUE

WED

THU

FRI

SAT

SUN

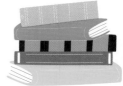

"Remember, you're not half of anything,
you're twice of everything."

VIET THANH NGUYEN, *THE SYMPATHIZER*

THE THINGS THEY CARRIED

TIM O'BRIEN

DATE STARTED	DATE FINISHED	MY RATING
		☆☆☆☆☆

"In the end...a true war story is never about war. It's about sunlight. It's about the special way that dawn spreads out on a river when you know you must cross the river and march into the mountains and do things you are afraid to. It's about love and memory. It's about sorrow. It's about sisters who never write back and people who never listen." In Tim O'Brien's world, a war story is all that—and more. This collection of twenty-two related stories has the cumulative effect of a unified novel. The "things they carry"—literally—are prosaic things: amphetamines, M-16s, grenades, good-luck charms, Sterno cans, toilet paper, photographs, C-rations. But the men in O'Brien's platoon—Curt Lemon, Rat Kiley, Henry Dobbins, Kiowa, and the rest—also carry less tangible but more palpable things such as disease, confusion, hatred, love, regret, fear, and what passes for courage.

What imperceptible things do you carry?

MON

TUE

WED

THU

FRI

SAT

SUN

"A thing may happen and be a total lie; another thing may not happen and be truer than the truth."

TIM O'BRIEN, *THE THINGS THEY CARRIED*

35

THERE THERE

TOMMY ORANGE

ANDREW CARNEGIE MEDAL FOR EXCELLENCE IN FICTION, 2019 FINALIST

DATE STARTED	DATE FINISHED	MY RATING
		☆☆☆☆☆

The upcoming Big Oakland Powwow brings together many at-first disconnected individuals. Some have been working on the event for months, some will sneak in with only good intentions, while others are plotting to steal the sizable cash prizes. Opal recalls occupying Alcatraz as a child with her family; today she raises her sister's grandchildren as her own after their unspeakable loss. With grant support, Dene endeavors to complete the oral-history project his deceased uncle couldn't, recording the stories of Indians living in Oakland. In his thirties, with his white mother's blessing, Edwin reaches out to the Native father he never met. Each of them wrestles with what it means to be Native American.

What are the most inspiring parts of your relatives' life stories?

THE WEEK OF ______________ – ______________

MON

TUE

WED

THU

FRI

SAT

SUN

"We are the memories we don't remember, which live in us, which we feel, which make us sing and dance and pray the way we do."

TOMMY ORANGE, *THERE THERE*

36

LOOKING FOR LORRAINE: THE RADIANT AND RADICAL LIFE OF LORRAINE HANSBERRY

IMANI PERRY

DATE STARTED	DATE FINISHED	MY RATING
		☆☆☆☆☆

"She sparked and sparkled," writes author Imani Perry of Lorraine Hansberry, who was all of twenty-nine when her best-known work, the Chicago-set play *A Raisin in the Sun*, opened on Broadway in 1959. Perry observes, "audiences had never before seen the work of a Black playwright and director, featuring a Black cast with no singing, dancing, or slapstick and a clear social message." In spite of Hansberry's subsequent celebrity, knowledge and understanding of her life and her varied and vital body of work have been limited at best. Mining writings private and published, collecting memories, tracking the reverberations of Hansberry's personality, words, and actions, and, at times, entering the narrative of this biography, Perry illuminates the thoughts, feelings, and revolutionary social consciousness of this brightly blazing artist, thinker, and activist.

**Think of someone who you consider a brightly blazing artist.
How do they inspire you?**

THE WEEK OF _____ – _____

MON

TUE

WED

THU

FRI

SAT

SUN

"Broadway audiences had never before seen
the work of a Black playwright and director,
featuring a Black cast with no singing, dancing,
or slapstick and a clear social message."

IMANI PERRY, *LOOKING FOR LORRAINE*

MONTH & YEAR: _____

SUNDAY	MONDAY	TUESDAY	WEDNESDAY

THURSDAY	FRIDAY	SATURDAY

MONTHLY GOALS

GOALS FOR THE MONTH AHEAD

WHAT WORKED LAST MONTH

FAVORITE BOOKS AND MOMENTS FROM LAST MONTH

READING IS HABIT

TRACK NEW HABITS & READING GOALS AND WATCH YOUR PROGRESS EVERY MONTH!

HABIT	1	2	3	4	5	6	7	8	9	10	11	12	13	14	15	16	17	18	19	20	21	22	23	24	25	26	27	28	29	30	31

37

JUST US: AN AMERICAN CONVERSATION

CLAUDIA RANKINE

ANDREW CARNEGIE MEDAL FOR EXCELLENCE IN NONFICTION, 2021 FINALIST

DATE STARTED	DATE FINISHED	MY RATING
		☆☆☆☆☆

Author Claudia Rankine analyzes the overwhelming power of whiteness in everyday interactions in this blend of essays and images. Whether it's the white airline passenger who steps confidently in front of her in the first-class line or a college friend who has no memory of a campus cross burning, whiteness erases Black lives and perceptions, stranding Black people in a nebulous gaslight dimension, their Blackness "a most disagreeable mirror." Touching on Beyoncé, blondness, skin lightening, and the inherent tensions in her own interracial marriage, Rankine opens a literary window into the Black experience for those willing to look in.

List three books you've read that have provided a window into the life experiences of someone different from you.

THE WEEK OF _____ – _____

MON

TUE

WED

THU

FRI

SAT

SUN

"I yearn to rise out of the restlessness of
my own forms of helplessness inside a
structure that constricts possibilities."

CLAUDIA RANKINE, *JUST US: AN AMERICAN CONVERSATION*

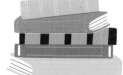

38

LINCOLN IN THE BARDO

GEORGE SAUNDERS

ANDREW CARNEGIE MEDAL FOR EXCELLENCE IN FICTION, 2018 FINALIST

DATE STARTED	DATE FINISHED	MY RATING
		☆☆☆☆☆

Anchored to a historic moment—the death of President Abraham Lincoln's young son, Willie, in February 1862—the surreal action in this story takes place in a cemetery when Lincoln enters the crypt to hold his boy's body one last time. Scenes of epic sorrow turn grotesque as a choir of specters, caught in the bardo—the mysterious transitional state following death and preceding rebirth, heaven, or hell—tell their stories, which range from the gleefully ribald to the tragic in tales embodying the dire conflicts underlying the then-raging Civil War in this macabre carnival of the dead.

What historic moment most intrigues you?

THE WEEK OF _____ – _____

MON

TUE

WED

THU

FRI

SAT

SUN

"These and all things started as nothing, latent within
a vast energy-broth, but then we named them, and
loved them, and, in this way, brought them forth."

GEORGE SAUNDERS, *LINCOLN IN THE BARDO*

SWING TIME

ZADIE SMITH

ANDREW CARNEGIE MEDAL FOR EXCELLENCE IN FICTION, 2017 FINALIST

39

DATE STARTED	DATE FINISHED	MY RATING
		☆☆☆☆☆

The unnamed narrator in this story is entranced and provoked by a Fred Astaire dance number in the movie *Swing Time*. Though passionate and knowledgeable about dance, especially pioneering African American tap stars Jeni LeGon and the Nicholas Brothers, the narrator doesn't have the body for it, while her child-hood best friend, Tracey, has the requisite build and drive. Both "brown girls" lived in a London housing project in the early 1980s—the narrator with her ambitiously political Jamaican mother and her laid-back white father, Tracey with her white mother, longing for her Black father whose appearances were infrequent and fraught. Close as they are, the girls are destined for diverging paths as Tracey stakes her future on dance, and the narrator muddles through a goth phase and college, then lucks into a job as a personal assistant to an international pop star, the fiercely willful, strikingly pale Aimee, who hijacks her life.

What art form inspires you the most?

THE WEEK OF ______________________ – __________________________

MON

TUE

WED

THU

FRI

SAT

SUN

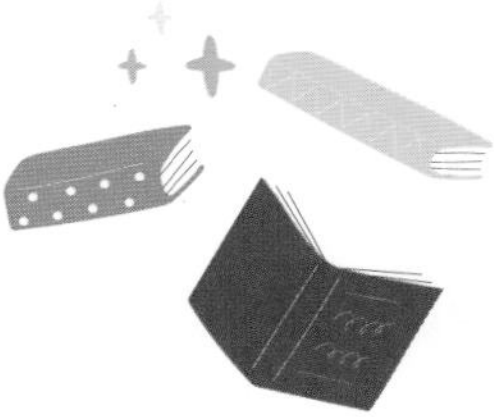

"I'd decided to establish a new rule for myself: read for half an hour an evening, no matter what."

ZADIE SMITH, *SWING TIME*

40

MAUS: A SURVIVOR'S TALE

ART SPIEGELMAN

DATE STARTED	DATE FINISHED	MY RATING
		☆☆☆☆☆

Author Art Spiegelman takes his own life for subject matter in this stunning addition to Holocaust literature. In *Maus: A Survivor's Tale*, he queries his cantankerous father about what it was like to live through the Nazi occupation of Poland and the death camps. This decidedly unfrivolous comic book is, first, the father's story and, second, the portrayal of the son's edgy relationship with the old man. In physical decline—Vladek Spiegelman has a harrowing heart seizure during one of their conversations—he seems permanently shocked by his experiences into a personal psychology of hardship. He can give nothing but his story. His son writes and draws it forcefully. He uses a simple iconographic device to evoke the terror of his father's times: the Jews all have mouse heads, the Germans those of cats.

Draw an icon of what you fear most.

MON

TUE

WED

THU

FRI

SAT

SUN

"No, darling! To die it's easy...
But you have to struggle for life!"

ART SPIEGELMAN, *MAUS: A SURVIVOR'S TALE*

41

JUST MERCY: A STORY OF JUSTICE AND REDEMPTION

BRYAN STEVENSON

ANDREW CARNEGIE MEDAL FOR EXCELLENCE IN NONFICTION, 2015 WINNER

DATE STARTED	DATE FINISHED	MY RATING
		☆☆☆☆☆

As a young Harvard law student testing himself in an internship in Georgia, author Bryan Stevenson visited death row inmates and saw firsthand the injustices suffered by the poor and disadvantaged, how too many had been railroaded into convictions with inadequate legal representation. The visit made such an impression on Stevenson that he started the Equal Justice Institute in Montgomery, Alabama. One of his first clients was Walter McMillian, a young Black man accused of murdering a white woman and imprisoned on death row even before he was tried. Stevenson alternates chapters on the shocking miscarriage of justice in McMillian's case, including police and prosecutorial misconduct, with other startling cases. Among the cases Stevenson cites: a fourteen-year-old condemned to death for killing his mother's abusive boyfriend and a mentally ill adolescent girl condemned to life in prison for second-degree murder for the death of young boys killed in a fire she started accidentally. Through these cases and others, Stevenson details changes in victims' rights, incarceration of juveniles, death penalty reforms, inflexible sentencing laws, and the continued practices of injustice that see too many juveniles, minorities, and mentally ill people imprisoned in a frenzy of mass incarceration in the United States.

How have you been inspired to help improve others' lives?

THE WEEK OF _____ – _____

MON

TUE

WED

THU

FRI

SAT

SUN

"Each of us is more than the worst
thing we've ever done."
BRYAN STEVENSON, *JUST MERCY*

MONTH & YEAR: _____

SUNDAY	MONDAY	TUESDAY	WEDNESDAY

THURSDAY	FRIDAY	SATURDAY

MONTHLY GOALS

GOALS FOR THE MONTH AHEAD

WHAT WORKED LAST MONTH

FAVORITE BOOKS AND MOMENTS FROM LAST MONTH

READING IS HABIT

TRACK NEW HABITS & READING GOALS AND WATCH YOUR PROGRESS EVERY MONTH!

HABIT	1	2	3	4	5	6	7	8	9	10	11	12	13	14	15	16	17	18	19	20	21	22	23	24	25	26	27	28	29	30	31

YOUNG MUNGO

DOUGLAS STUART

42

DATE STARTED	DATE FINISHED	MY RATING
		☆☆☆☆☆

Mungo is a fifteen-year-old living in Glasgow. The youngest son of an alcoholic mother, Mungo would do anything "just to make other people feel better." He is a gentle soul living in an environment of toxic masculinity, sectarian violence, and drink, but he has strong reserves of strength that he himself doesn't know he possesses. Love for another young man would be risky, but when Mungo, a Protestant, falls in love with James, a Catholic, the peril is immense. Will Mungo be true to himself in a place that demands conformity to social and gender rules?

Write about a time you defied the demands to conform.

THE WEEK OF _____ – _____

MON

TUE

WED

THU

FRI

SAT

SUN

"He hadn't known that the sky could hold so many hues—or he hadn't paid it any mind before. Did anyone in Glasgow look up?"

DOUGLAS STUART, *YOUNG MUNGO*

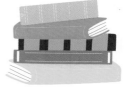

43

ALL MY RAGE
SABAA TAHIR

DATE STARTED	DATE FINISHED	MY RATING
		☆☆☆☆☆

Estranged friends Salahudin and Noor are finding their way back to each other—or not—in the wake of Salahudin's mother's death. Salahudin is confronted with the possibility of the loss of the family motel and Noor with the loss of the future she's dreamed about ever since surviving an earthquake in Pakistan. Both are forced to make difficult choices that will retest their already shaky relationship.

**Write about an experience that tested a friendship.
What happened, and how did it change you?**

THE WEEK OF _____ — _____

MON

TUE

WED

THU

FRI

SAT

SUN

"Great passions grow into monsters in the dark of the mind; but if you share them with loving friends they remain human, they can be endured."

SABAA TAHIR, *ALL MY RAGE*

THE GOLDFINCH

DONNA TARTT

ANDREW CARNEGIE MEDAL FOR EXCELLENCE IN FICTION, 2014 WINNER

44

DATE STARTED	DATE FINISHED	MY RATING
		☆☆☆☆☆

In the wake of his nefarious father's abandonment, Theo, a smart, thirteen-year-old Manhattanite, is extremely close to his vivacious mother—until an act of terrorism catapults him into a dizzying world bereft of gravity, certainty, or love. Theo first seeks sanctuary with a troubled Park Avenue family and, in Greenwich Village, with a kind and gifted restorer of antique furniture. Fate then delivers Theo to utterly alien Las Vegas, where he meets young outlaw Boris. As Theo, stricken with grief and post-traumatic stress disorder, becomes a complexly damaged adult, he is pulled into the shadowlands of art, lashed to seventeenth-century Dutch artist Carel Fabritius and his exquisite if sinister painting, *The Goldfinch*.

Is there a piece of art you are connected to or moved by?

THE WEEK OF ______________________ – ______________________

MON

TUE

WED

THU

FRI

SAT

SUN

"To understand the world at all, sometimes you could only focus on a tiny bit of it, look very hard at what was close to hand and make it stand in for the whole."

DONNA TARTT, *THE GOLDFINCH*

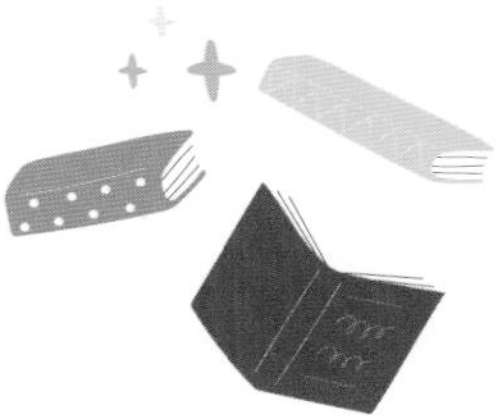

45

THE HATE U GIVE
ANGIE THOMAS

DATE STARTED	DATE FINISHED	MY RATING
		☆☆☆☆☆

Sixteen-year-old Starr lives in two very different worlds: one is her home in a poor Black urban neighborhood; the other is the tony suburban prep school she attends and the white boy she dates there. Her bifurcated life changes dramatically when she is the only witness to the unprovoked police shooting of her unarmed friend Khalil and is challenged to speak out—though with trepidation—about the injustices being done in the event's wake. As the case becomes national news, violence erupts in her neighborhood, and Starr finds herself and her family caught in the middle. Difficulties are exacerbated by their encounters with the local drug lord for whom Khalil was dealing to earn money for his impoverished family. If there is to be hope for change, Starr comes to realize, it must be through the exercise of her voice, even if it puts her and her family in harm's way.

How can you use your voice to promote social justice?

THE WEEK OF _____ – _____

MON

TUE

WED

THU

FRI

SAT

SUN

"What's the point of having a voice
if you're gonna be silent in those
moments you shouldn't be?"

ANGIE THOMAS, *THE HATE U GIVE*

MONTH & YEAR: _____

SUNDAY	MONDAY	TUESDAY	WEDNESDAY

THURSDAY	FRIDAY	SATURDAY

MONTHLY GOALS

GOALS FOR THE MONTH AHEAD

WHAT WORKED LAST MONTH

FAVORITE BOOKS AND MOMENTS FROM LAST MONTH

READING IS HABIT

TRACK NEW HABITS & READING GOALS AND WATCH YOUR PROGRESS EVERY MONTH!

HABIT	1	2	3	4	5	6	7	8	9	10	11	12	13	14	15	16	17	18	19	20	21	22	23	24	25	26	27	28	29	30	31

46

THE CLIMATE BOOK: THE FACTS AND THE SOLUTIONS

GRETA THUNBERG

DATE STARTED	DATE FINISHED	MY RATING
		☆☆☆☆☆

Thunberg was just eight years old when she became existentially aware of environmental distress. By fifteen, she was leading protests outside Sweden's parliament and speaking to the UN. At sixteen, she received her first Nobel Peace Prize nomination. Thunberg's commitment to global education regarding the perils of climate change manifests itself in this sweeping compendium of essays contributed by more than one hundred academicians, authors, environmentalists, and journalists whose specific professional expertise or profound humanitarian concern amplifies the existing science surrounding this crisis of sustainability and ecology.

What were you passionate about as an eight-year-old?
What steps did you plan to take to address the issue?

THE WEEK OF _____ – _____

MON

TUE

WED

THU

FRI

SAT

SUN

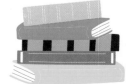

"Science is a tool, and we all need
to learn how to use it."

GRETA THUNBERG, *THE CLIMATE BOOK*

NORA WEBSTER

COLM TÓIBÍN

ANDREW CARNEGIE MEDAL FOR EXCELLENCE IN FICTION, 2015 FINALIST

47

DATE STARTED	DATE FINISHED	MY RATING
		☆☆☆☆☆

With the early death of her beloved Maurice, fortysomething Nora Webster becomes a widow with four children and scarcely enough money to cover the family expenses. Nora must step out of the rather cocoon-like world she and her husband had created for themselves in the small city of Wexford, Ireland. "The problem for her was that she was on her own now and that she had no idea how to live." Her sisters, aunts, and friends all offer assistance and advice as she navigates unfamiliar terrain. Can she put the memory of Maurice to the side and create a new life?

Describe a bold, independent, and fierce woman you know.

THE WEEK OF _____ – _____

MON

TUE

WED

THU

FRI

SAT

SUN

"So turn back now before the fog comes down so hard that you won't be able to drive home."

COLM TÓIBÍN, *NORA WEBSTER*

48

MEMORIAL DRIVE: A DAUGHTER'S MEMOIR

NATASHA TRETHEWEY

ANDREW CARNEGIE MEDAL FOR EXCELLENCE IN NONFICTION, 2021 FINALIST

DATE STARTED	DATE FINISHED	MY RATING
		☆☆☆☆☆

In her memoir, Pulitzer Prize–winning poet Natasha Trethewey confronts the horror of her mother's murder. Trethewey's white Canadian father and her Black American mother met in college and eloped, their 1966 marriage deemed illegal in Mississippi. Trethewey recounts her sunny childhood within the embrace of her mother's accomplished and valiant extended family. Shadows grow after her parents divorced and Trethewey and her mother, Gwendolyn, moved to Atlanta, where Gwendolyn earned a graduate degree in social work while supporting them as a waitress. Enter dangerously unbalanced Joel. When Gwendolyn finally broke free from him, she secured police protection, but it proved to be catastrophically inadequate. Through finely honed, ever more harrowing memories, dreams, visions, and musings, Trethewey maps the inexorable path to her mother's murder.

What have you gained from reading memoirs?

THE WEEK OF ______ – ______

MON

TUE

WED

THU

FRI

SAT

SUN

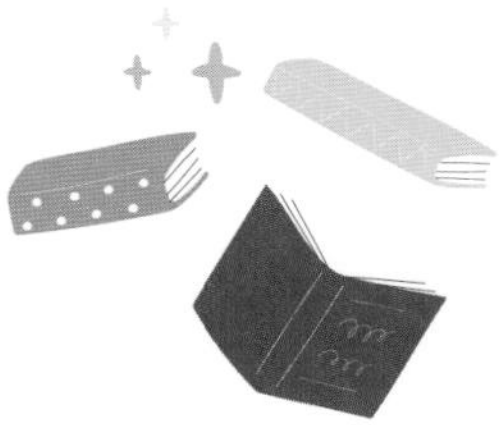

"What matters is the transformative power of metaphor and the stories we tell ourselves about the arc and meaning of our lives."

NATASHA TRETHEWEY, *MEMORIAL DRIVE*

49

THE HEARTBEAT OF WOUNDED KNEE: NATIVE AMERICA FROM 1890 TO THE PRESENT

DAVID TREUER

ANDREW CARNEGIE MEDAL FOR EXCELLENCE IN NONFICTION, 2020 FINALIST

DATE STARTED	DATE FINISHED	MY RATING
		☆☆☆☆☆

David Treuer—acclaimed Ojibwe author and professor from the Leech Lake Reservation in northern Minnesota—here offers his own very personal counternarrative to the depressing story of defeated, hopeless Native Americans depicted in Dee Brown's 1970 classic, *Bury My Heart at Wounded Knee*. Treuer guides the reader along the path of Native history since that 1890 massacre, not just highlighting the ways in which treaties were ignored, how the disastrous policy of assimilation was aimed at wiping out centuries of culture and language, and the drastic reduction of Indian land holdings resulting from the Dawes Act of 1877, but focusing instead on how each of these assaults on everything Indigenous people held dear actually led to their strong resolve not only to survive but to emerge reenergized.

Write about resolve and reinvention in your own life.

MON

TUE

WED

THU

FRI

SAT

SUN

"They survived to make mistakes and to recover from them. They survived to make history, to make meaning, to make life."

DAVID TREUER, *THE HEARTBEAT OF WOUNDED KNEE*

ON EARTH WE'RE BRIEFLY GORGEOUS

OCEAN VUONG

50

DATE STARTED	DATE FINISHED	MY RATING
		☆☆☆☆☆

Little Dog, a Vietnamese refugee, grew up in Hartford with his mother and his maternal grandmother, Lan. Now a writer, Little Dog frames his story as a letter to his mother, who cannot read, "to tell you everything you'll never know." He recalls her painful attempts to toughen him and his simultaneous rage for all that frays her—work, memories, difficulty communicating. At fourteen, he gets a job cutting tobacco and there meets Trevor. Two years older, Trevor works to escape his alcoholic father and makes Little Dog feel "seen—I who had seldom been seen by anyone." Their covert love blooms brilliantly as Trevor, battling his own demons, handles Little Dog with bewildering warmth.

Who in your life sees you most clearly,
and what does that mean to you?

THE WEEK OF _____ – _____

MON

TUE

WED

THU

FRI

SAT

SUN

"Remember: The rules, like the streets,
can only take you to known places."

OCEAN VUONG, *ON EARTH WE'RE BRIEFLY GORGEOUS*

MONTH & YEAR: _____

SUNDAY	MONDAY	TUESDAY	WEDNESDAY

THURSDAY	FRIDAY	SATURDAY

MONTHLY GOALS

GOALS FOR THE MONTH AHEAD

WHAT WORKED LAST MONTH

FAVORITE BOOKS AND MOMENTS FROM LAST MONTH

READING IS HABIT

TRACK NEW HABITS & READING GOALS AND WATCH YOUR PROGRESS EVERY MONTH!

HABIT	1	2	3	4	5	6	7	8	9	10	11	12	13	14	15	16	17	18	19	20	21	22	23	24	25	26	27	28	29	30	31

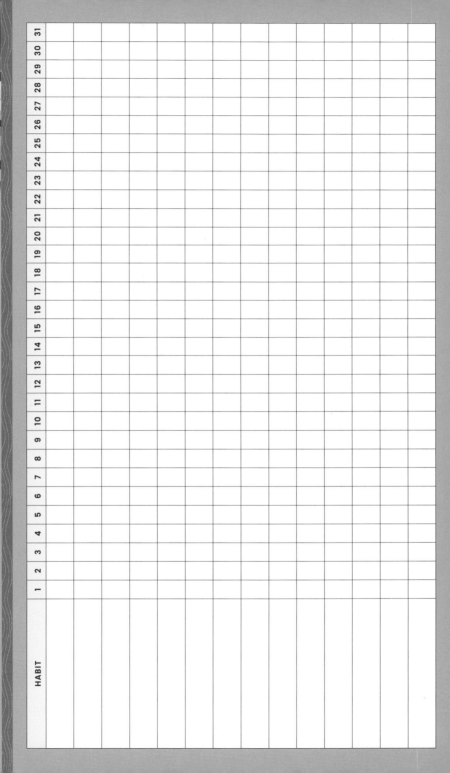

51

THE UNDERGROUND RAILROAD

COLSON WHITEHEAD

ANDREW CARNEGIE MEDAL FOR EXCELLENCE IN FICTION, 2017 WINNER

DATE STARTED	DATE FINISHED	MY RATING
		☆☆☆☆☆

Smart and resilient Cora, a young third-generation enslaved girl on a Georgia cotton plantation, has been brutally attacked by whites and Blacks. Certain that the horror will only get worse, she flees with a young man who knows how to reach the Underground Railroad, an actual railroad running through tunnels dug beneath the blood-soaked fields of the South. Yet freedom proves miserably elusive. A South Carolina town appears to be welcoming until Cora discovers that it is all a facade, concealing quasi-medical genocidal schemes. With a notoriously relentless bounty hunter following close behind, Cora endures another terrifying underground journey, arriving in North Carolina, where the corpses of tortured Black people hang on the trees along a road whites call the Freedom Trail. Each stop Cora makes along the Underground Railroad reveals another shocking and malignant symptom of a country riven by catastrophic conflicts, a poisonous moral crisis, and diabolical violence.

Write about an unforgettable journey you've taken.
How did it change you as a person?

THE WEEK OF _____ – _____

MON

TUE

WED

THU

FRI

SAT   **SUN**

"Truth was a changing display in a shop
window, manipulated by hands when you weren't
looking, alluring and ever out of reach."

COLSON WHITEHEAD, *THE UNDERGROUND RAILROAD*

52

A LITTLE LIFE
HANYA YANAGIHARA
ANDREW CARNEGIE MEDAL FOR EXCELLENCE IN FICTION, 2016 FINALIST

DATE STARTED	DATE FINISHED	MY RATING
		☆☆☆☆☆

Four college men move to New York to start their adult lives. They include Malcolm, a light-skinned African American architect from a wealthy background; JB, an occasional drug-using artist of Haitian ancestry; Willem, the handsome actor who, as we first meet him, is of course waiting tables downtown; and, at center stage, Jude. Although Jude is a successful litigator, he is frail, vulnerable, private, and given to self-harm. In his neediness, he is the focus of the others' existence.

How do you support your friends in achieving their ambitions?

THE WEEK OF _____ – _____

MON

TUE

WED

THU

FRI

SAT

SUN

"Wasn't friendship its own miracle, the finding
of another person who made the entire lonely
world seem somehow less lonely?"

HANYA YANAGIHARA, *A LITTLE LIFE*

AN IMMENSE WORLD: HOW ANIMAL SENSES REVEAL THE HIDDEN REALMS AROUND US

ED YONG

ANDREW CARNEGIE MEDAL FOR EXCELLENCE IN NONFICTION, 2023 WINNER

53

DATE STARTED	DATE FINISHED	MY RATING
		☆☆☆☆☆

The distinctive sensory experiences, "sensescapes," of different animals can be dominated not just by vision, smell, taste, touch, or sound but also heat, flow, and even magnetoreception. The platypus has a bill that detects electric fields, sand scorpions rely on surface vibrations to hunt prey, killer flies have ultrafast vision, and the tongue of a slithering rattlesnake "turns the world into both map and menu." The menagerie of critters on earth—humans included—have particular perceptual abilities and perceive only a portion of our immense world.

**Write from the perspective of a small animal or insect.
What does the world look like through their eyes?**

THE WEEK OF ______ – ______

MON

TUE

WED

THU

FRI

SAT

SUN

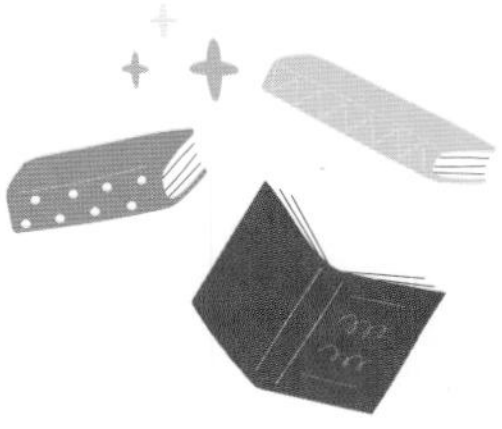

"To perceive the world through other senses is to find splendor in familiarity, and the sacred in the mundane."

ED YONG, *AN IMMENSE WORLD*

FOUR TREASURES OF THE SKY

JENNY TINGHUI ZHANG

DATE STARTED	DATE FINISHED	MY RATING
		☆☆☆☆☆

As a child in China, Daiyu resents being named after Lin Daiyu, a tragic heroine; she promises herself that she will never be so weak. On her own at twelve, she passes as a boy and finds work at a calligraphy school until she is kidnapped and trafficked to the United States. Fleeing from a San Francisco brothel, she reinvents herself again as a young man named Jacob and finds relative security and friendship in a town in the mountains of Idaho. But as anti-Chinese sentiment spreads across the American West, Daiyu is forced not only to reckon with the legacy of her namesake but also to find a way to integrate all of her identities.

What does your name mean to you?

THE WEEK OF _____ – _____

MON

TUE

WED

THU

FRI

SAT

SUN

"There is no such thing as luck, I told him.
Luck is just readiness that meets opportunity."

JENNY TINGHUI ZHANG, *FOUR TREASURES OF THE SKY*

CURRENT READS

TITLE	START	FINISH	RATING

TITLE	START	FINISH	RATING

TITLE	START	FINISH	RATING

TITLE	START	FINISH	RATING

TITLE	START	FINISH	RATING

TITLE	START	FINISH	RATING

TITLE	START	FINISH	RATING

TITLE	START	FINISH	RATING

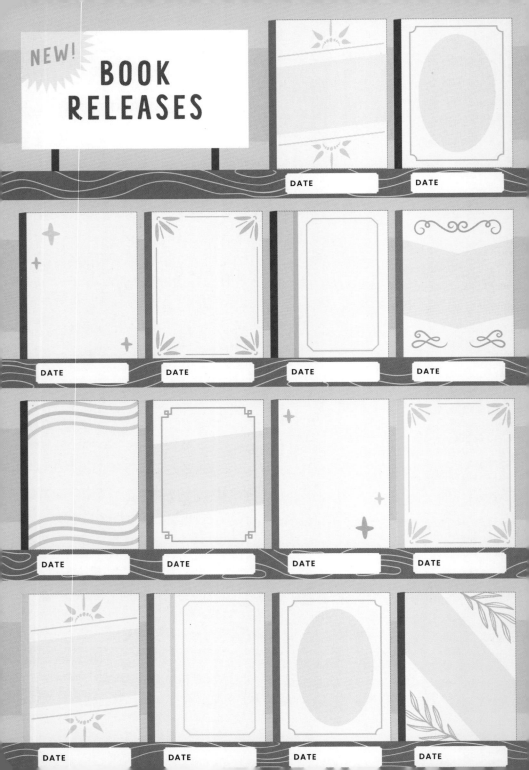

NEW!

BOOK
RELEASES

DATE

DATE

DATE

DATE

DATE

DATE

DATE

DATE

DATE

DATE

DATE

DATE

DATE

DATE

DATE

DATE

DATE

DATE

DATE

DATE

DATE

DATE

DATE

DATE

DATE

DATE

DATE

DATE

DATE

DATE

DATE

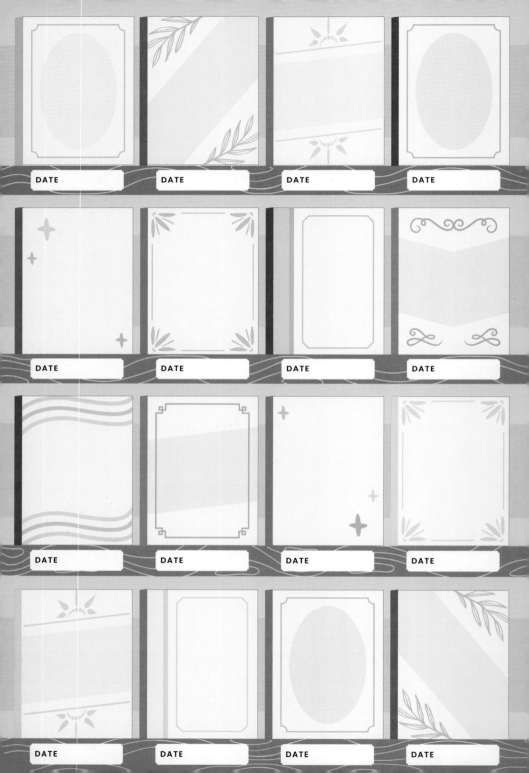

DATE

DATE

DATE

DATE

DATE

DATE

DATE

DATE

DATE

DATE

DATE

DATE

DATE

DATE

DATE

DATE

DATE

DATE

DATE

DATE

DATE

DATE

DATE

DATE

DATE

DATE

DATE

DATE

DATE

DATE

DATE

DATE

MY WISHLIST

TITLE	AUTHOR

TITLE	AUTHOR

TITLE	AUTHOR

TITLE	AUTHOR

BOOKS I OWN

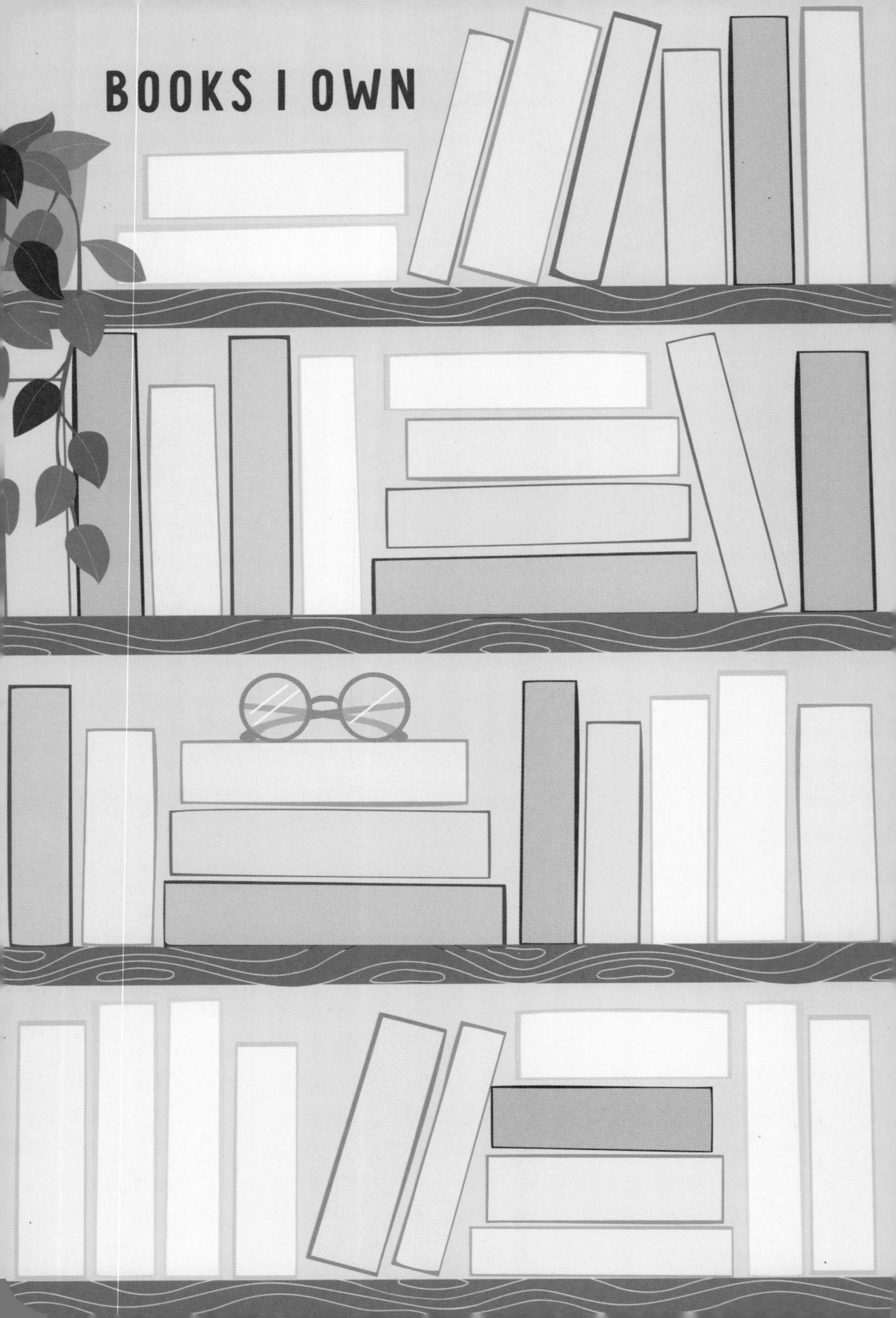

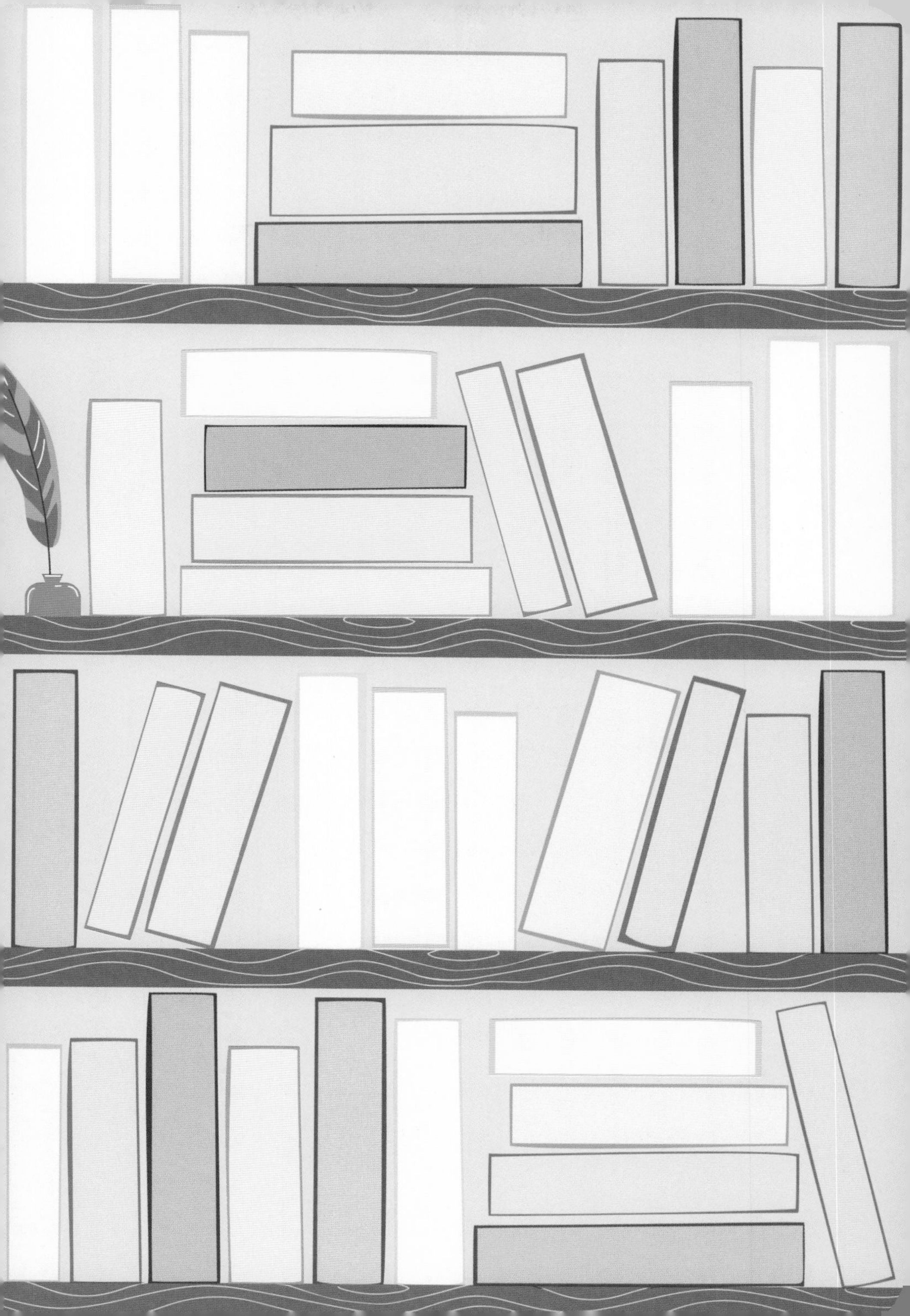

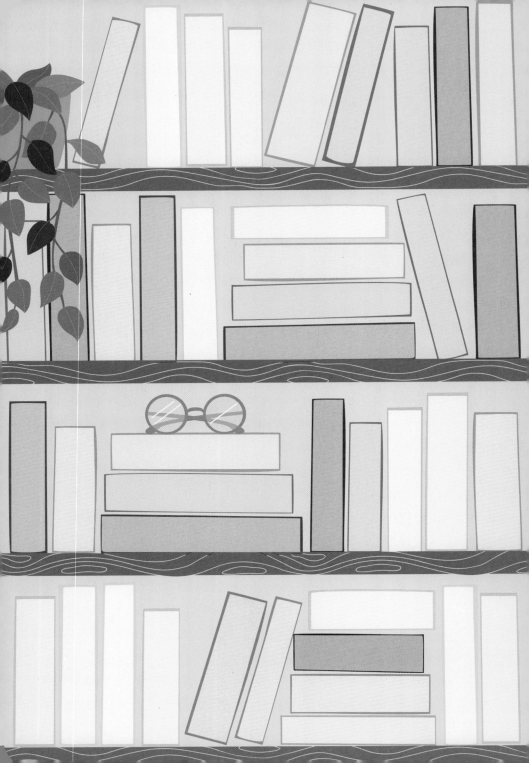

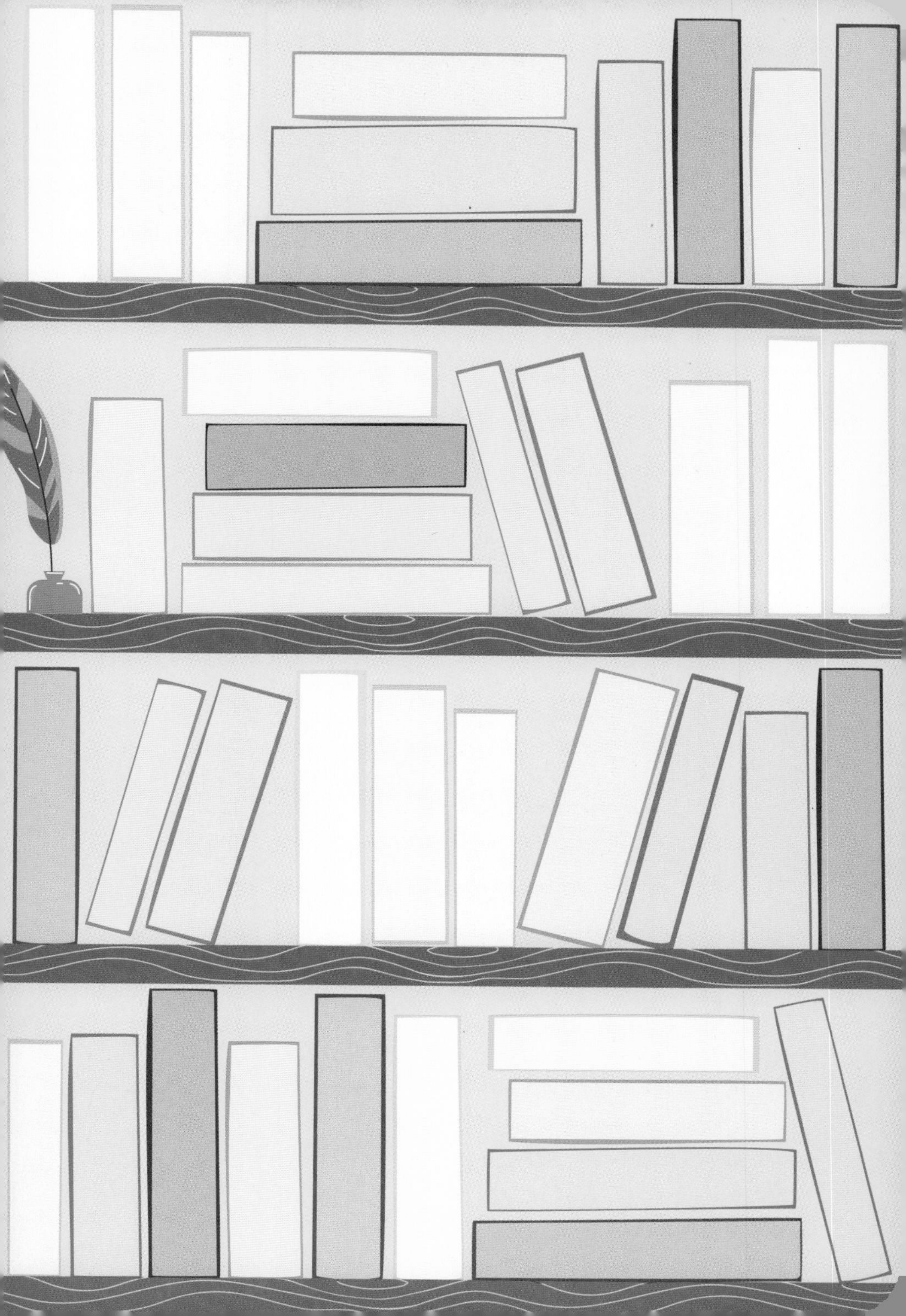

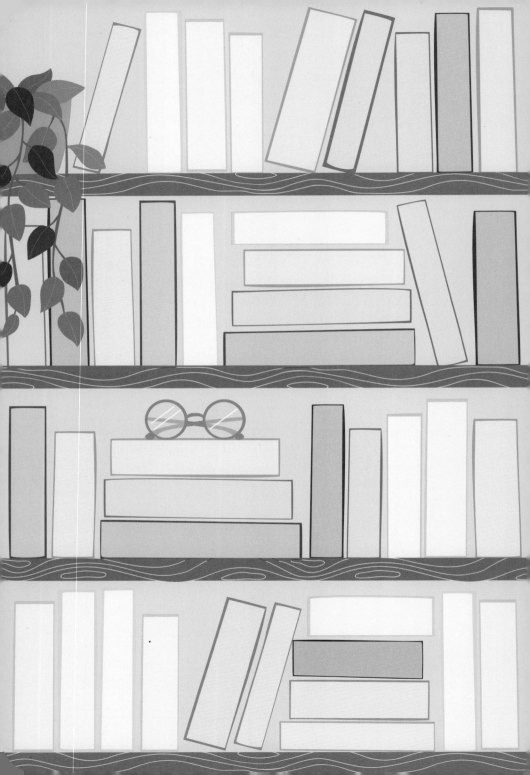

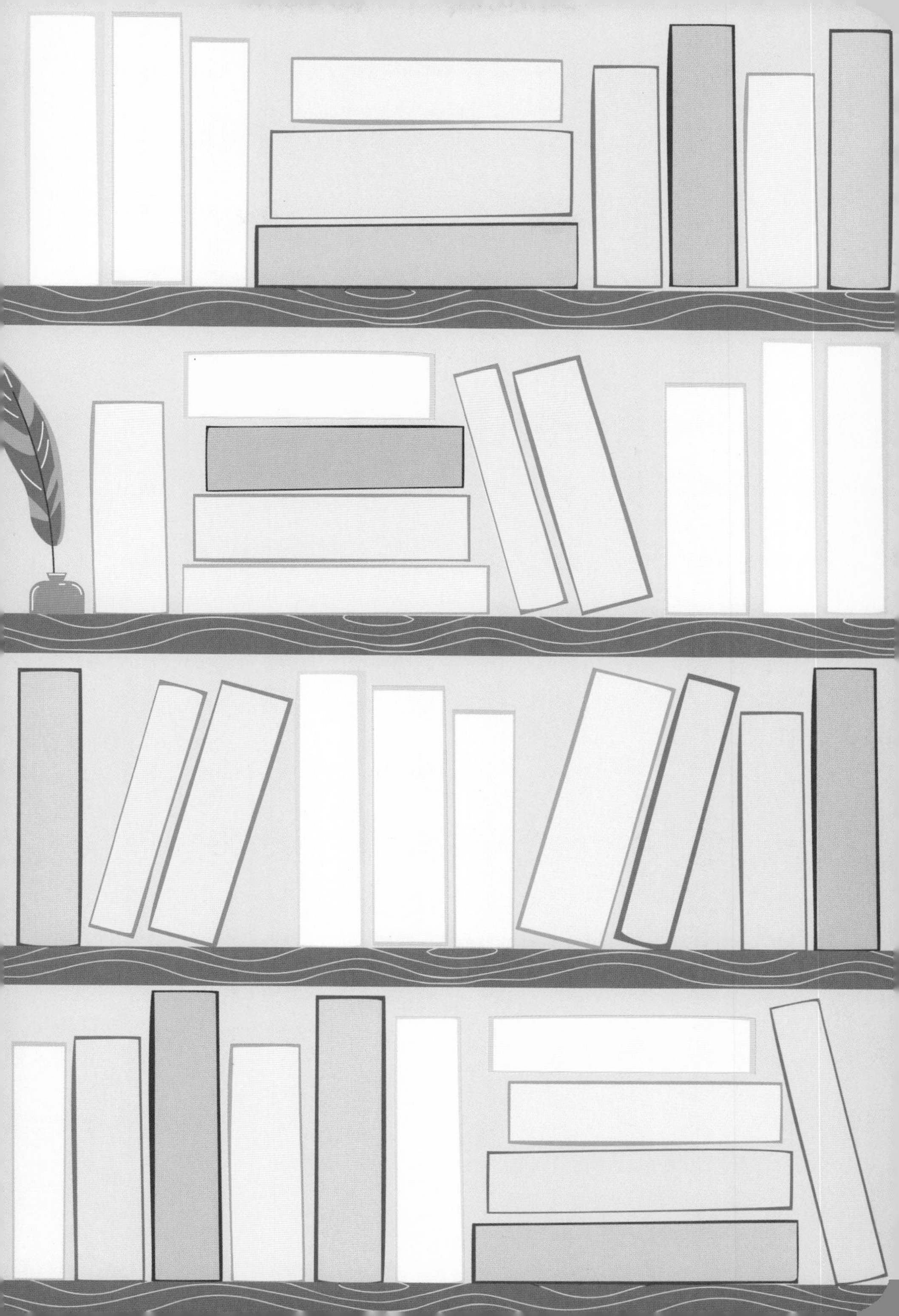

LIBRARY BOOKS

TITLE	AUTHOR	CHECKED OUT	DUE	RETURNED?

TITLE	AUTHOR	CHECKED OUT	DUE	RETURNED?

TITLE	AUTHOR	CHECKED OUT	DUE	RETURNED?

TITLE	AUTHOR	CHECKED OUT	DUE	RETURNED?

FAVORITE READS

TITLE	WHY?

TITLE	WHY?

TITLE	WHY?

TITLE	WHY?

NOTES

The reviews come from *Booklist*. *Booklist* is the book review magazine of the American Library Association and is a vibrant source of reading recommendations for all readers. It's been considered an essential collection development and readers' advisory tool by thousands of librarians for more than 100 years. For more info, visit booklistonline.com.

Published by Sourcebooks
P.O. Box 4410, Naperville, Illinois 60567-4410
(630)961-3900
sourcebooks.com

Printed and bound in China.
OGP 10 9 8 7 6 5 4 3 2 1